CIVIL WAR CHRONICLES

THE
UNDERGROUND RAILROAD

By Ruth Ashby

iBooks for Young Readers

For Ernie   —R.A.

Published by iBooks
an imprint of J. Boylston & Company, Publishers
www.ibooksinc.com
Produced by Byron Preiss Visual Publications, Inc.

Library of Congress Cataloging-in-Publication Data
Ashby, Ruth.
The Underground Railroad / by Ruth Ashby
v. cm. — (Civil War Chronicles)
Summary: Discusses the history of the institution of slavery in the United States,
abolitionism and other resistance movements, and the structure, as well as some
outstanding people involved with, the Underground Railroad.
ISBN 978-1-59687-515-9
1. Underground railroad—Juvenile literature. 2. Fugitive slaves—United States—
History—19th century—Juvenile literature. 3. Antislavery movements—United States—
History—19th century—Juvenile literature. [1. Underground railroad. 2. Fugitive slaves.
3. Antislavery movements.] I. Title.

E450 .A84 2002
973.7'115—dc21   2002017638

Second Edition

Contents

Introduction

The Civil War was the great American tragedy. From 1861 to 1865, it divided states, broke up families, took the lives of more than half a million people, and left much of the country in ruins. But it also abolished the great national shame of slavery and cleared the way for the astounding expansion of American industry and culture in the second half of the 19th century. Without the war, the United States would not have been so progressive or so united—and millions of its people would still have been in chains. In the end it was, perhaps, a necessary tragedy.

The conflict had loomed for decades. From the Constitutional Convention in 1787 on, the North and South disagreed about whether slavery should exist in the United States. In the North, slavery was gradually abolished between 1780 and 1827. But the South became ever more yoked to slavery as its economy became more dependent on the production of cotton. In the meantime, the United States was expanding westward. Every time a territory became a new state, the government had to decide whether it would be slave or free. For 40 years, Congress reached compromise after compromise.

Finally, differences could no longer be bandaged over. With the election of Republican Abraham Lincoln to the presidency in 1860, a crisis was reached. Southern states were afraid that Lincoln, who opposed slavery in the territories, would try to abolish it in the South as well—and that their economy and way of life would be destroyed.

✉ Abraham Lincoln

✉ Jefferson Davis

Robert E. Lee ✖

Ulysses S. Grant ✖

On December 20, 1860, South Carolina seceded from the Union. It was followed by Alabama, Florida, Georgia, Louisiana, Mississippi, Texas, Virginia, North Carolina, Tennessee, and Arkansas.

The rebellious states formed a new nation, the Confederate States of America, and elected a president, Jefferson Davis. On April 12, 1861, Confederate forces fired on the Federal post of Fort Sumter in Charleston Harbor—and the Civil War began. It lasted four years and touched the lives of every man, woman, and child in the nation. There were heroes on both sides, in the army and on the home front, from Union general Ulysses S. Grant and Confederate general Robert E. Lee to black leader Harriet Tubman and poet and nurse Walt Whitman. It is estimated that at least 620,000 soldiers were killed, almost as many Americans as in all other armed conflicts combined. When Lincoln issued the Emancipation Proclamation on January 1, 1863 and freed the slaves in the rebellious states, it became not just a war for reunification but a war of liberation as well.

Slavery and the Underground Railroad tells the story of the courageous men and women who escaped from slavery before and during the war, and of the determined people who helped them find freedom.

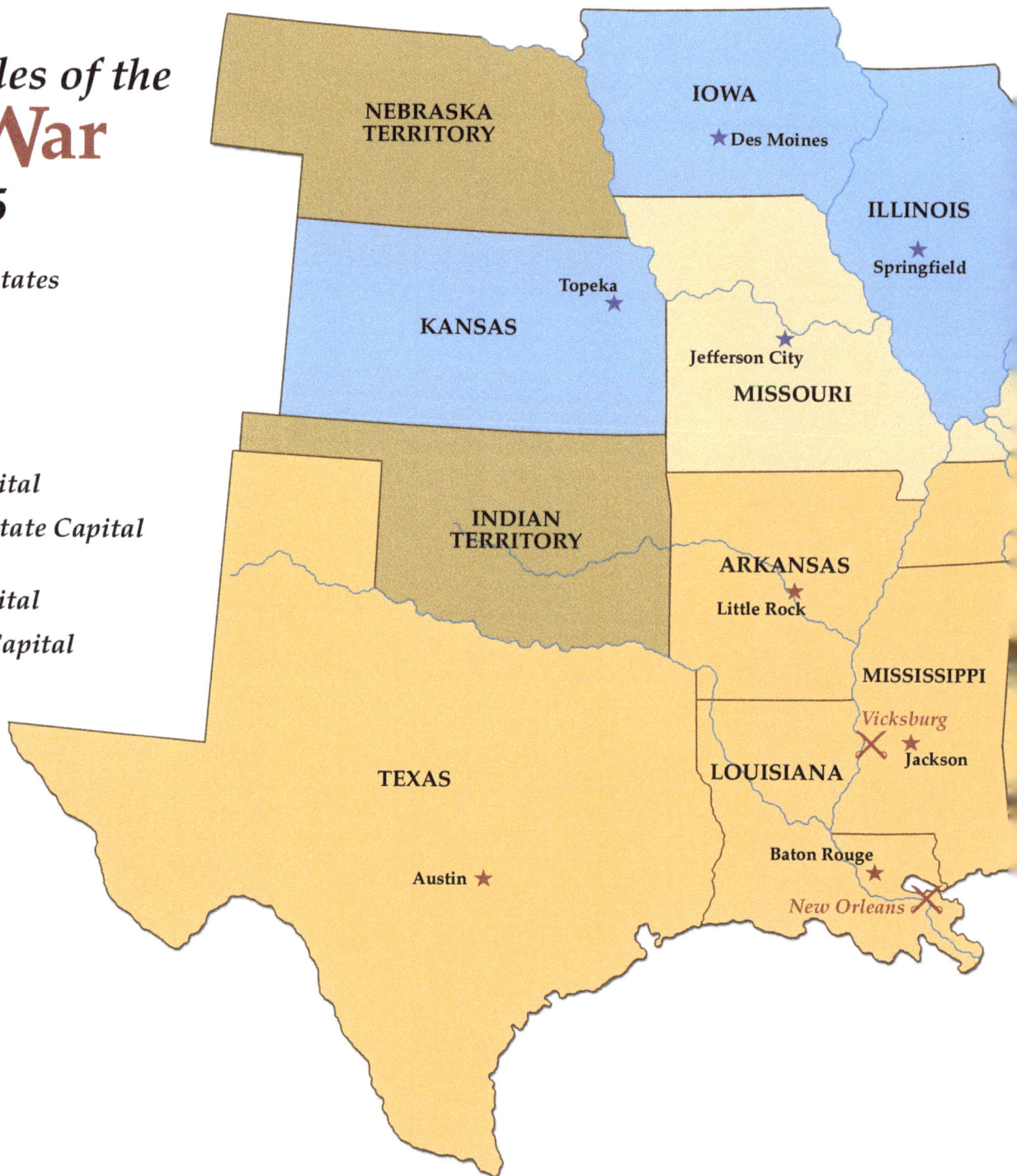

Major Battles of the
Civil War
1861 - 1865

- Confederate States
- Union States
- Border States
- Territories
- ⊛ Confederate National Capital
- ★ Confederate State Capital
- ⊛ Union National Capital
- ★ Union State Capital
- ✕ Battle Sites

NEBRASKA TERRITORY

IOWA
★ Des Moines

ILLINOIS
★ Springfield

KANSAS
Topeka ★

Jefferson City ★
MISSOURI

INDIAN TERRITORY

ARKANSAS
Little Rock ★

MISSISSIPPI
Vicksburg ✕ ★ Jackson

TEXAS

LOUISIANA

Austin ★

Baton Rouge ★

New Orleans ✕

INDIANA
Indianapolis

OHIO
Columbus

PENNSYLVANIA
Harrisburg
Gettysburg
Antietam

NEW JERSEY
Trenton

WEST VIRGINIA
Charleston

Washington, D.C.
Annapolis
Dover
DELAWARE
MARYLAND

KENTUCKY
Frankfort

VIRGINIA
(enlarged below)
Richmond

Fort Donelson
TENNESSEE
Nashville

NORTH CAROLINA
Raleigh

Shiloh
Chattanooga
Chickamauga

Columbia
SOUTH CAROLINA

Atlanta

ALABAMA
Montgomery

GEORGIA
Milledgeville

Fort Sumter

Savannah

Tallahassee

Mobile Bay

FLORIDA

BATTLES (on map below)

1 *Gettysburg*
2 *Antietam*
3 *Shenandoah Campaign*
4 *First and Second Manassas*
5 *Wilderness*
6 *Fredericksburg*
7 *Spotsylvania*
8 *Chancellorsville*
9 *Cold Harbor*
10 *Seven Days' Battles*
11 *Petersburg*
12 *Peninsular Campaign*
13 *First and Second Hampton Roads*

PENNSYLVANIA
1
MARYLAND
2
Washington, D.C.
Annapolis

WEST VIRGINIA
admitted to the Union June 20, 1863
3
4

5 6 7
8

VIRGINIA

Richmond 9
10
Appomattox
11
12
13

Chained slaves being taken across the Sahara.
Arabs sold African slaves for centuries before the
European slave trade began, but it didn't take
Europeans long to catch up.

Chapter One

The Peculiar Institution

In 1619, about 20 Africans came ashore in the new English settlement of Jamestown, Virginia. They were sold by Dutch traders to Virginian colonists to help plant and harvest tobacco. This was the beginning of slavery in the American colonies.

At first, slavery was not regulated. In the 1600s, some free black men were able to own property and even to vote in Virginia. But by 1723, free Africans could not vote. The number of slaves in the English colonies continued to grow, fueled by the lucrative triangular slave

Slaves aboard a slave ship. ⊠ During the trip from Africa to the Americas, slaves were crammed so tightly into the hold they could barely move.

trade between New England, Africa, and the West Indies. By 1776, there were some 500,000 slaves in the 13 American colonies that rebelled against England.

Most slaves lived in the South, where, in addition to working on rice and tobacco plantations, they held jobs along the seacoast, building ships and madng sails, ropes, and barrels. Africans who lived in the North usually inhabited cities like New York, Newport, and Philadelphia. By the time of the American Revolution, slavery was declining in the North. Many states voted to eliminate slavery, including New Hampshire, Vermont, Massachusetts, and Pennsylvania. By 1804, the rest of the Northern states had also made arrangements to phase slavery out. In New York, the last enslaved persons were set free in 1827.

It was a different story in the South, where the economy was largely dependent on slavery. Founding Fathers like George Washington,

Quick Facts

★ In the Three-Fifths Compromise at the Constitutional Convention in 1787, slaves were counted as three-fifths of a person in a state's population count. This way, Southern states with large slave populations would have a greater number of representatives in Congress.

★ In 1790, the United States produced about 3,000 bales of cotton (a bale weighs 500 pounds [227 kg]). After the introduction of the cotton gin in 1801, production rose to 100,000 bales. In 1860, it was four million bales. By the time of the Civil War,

✉ Slaves hoeing a cotton field.

Eli Whitney, a young ⊠ Connecticut schoolteacher, invented a new machine to clean cotton on a trip to Georgia in 1793. His invention revolutionized the production of cotton in the South.

The cotton gin separated the ⊠ cotton fiber from the seeds by feeding the cotton bolls through a rotating cylinder. Using the gin, a worker could clean up to 50 pounds (22.7 kg) of cotton a day.

Thomas Jefferson, and James Madison disliked slavery and hoped it would eventually disappear on its own. But at the Constitutional Convention in 1787, Southern states insisted a clause be written into the Constitution that continued the slave trade for the next 20 years. Article 1, Section 9 reads: "The Migration or Importation of such Persons as any of the States now existing shall think proper to admit, shall not be prohibited by the Congress prior to the Year one thousand eight hundred and eight. . . . " Also, Article 4, Section 2 of the Constitution indicated that fugitive slaves in free states should be returned to their masters.

And so, in the new country founded on the principles of "Life, Liberty, and the pursuit of Happiness," hundreds of thousands, and then millions, of people were in chains.

In 1808, the slave trade to the United States was outlawed, but slavery remained a cornerstone of the American plantation system. In 1793, Eli Whitney had invented the cotton gin. It cleaned cotton quickly, making

⊠ Slaves work on a Kentucky tobacco plantation in 1856.

it profitable for planters to grow huge crops to sell to the new textile factories in New England and Great Britain. Now planters needed large populations of workers to pick the cotton. Although some slaves were still imported illegally, most slave owners depended on "breeding" to multiply their slaves. The slave population grew as slave women had children and these children became slaves themselves. By 1860, there were some four million slaves worth $2 billion living in the South. The South was completely dependent on what was known as its "peculiar institution."

To control the millions of nonfree people within their borders, Southern states passed what were called "slave codes." "The slave should know that his master is to govern absolutely and he is to obey implicitly," one South Carolina law read. "That he is never for a moment to exercise either his will or judgment in opposition to a positive order." In all Southern states, it was a crime for slaves to learn how to read or write and for anyone to teach them. Slaves could not own guns, smoke tobacco, or hold meetings for fear they might be planning a revolt. If a slave left his master's home without a pass, patrollers called "paddy rollers" would hunt him down. Some owners even forbade their slaves to attend church services without supervision.

Slave owners used racism to justify slavery. Africans, they said, were savages, inferior to whites. Slavery was a natural institution, approved by the Bible and sanctioned by God. In this view, whites were actually doing blacks a favor by subjecting them. Africans were "untaught in all the useful arts and occupations, reared in heathen darkness; and sold by heathen masters," Confederate president Jefferson Davis once wrote. "They were transferred to shores enlightened by the rays of Christianity. . . . They increased from a few unprofitable savages to millions of efficient Christian laborers."

The "efficient laborers" led a harsh life. After he had escaped to a free state, black leader Frederick Douglass remembered that when he was enslaved, "we were worked in all weathers. It was never too hot or too cold; it could never rain, blow, hail, or snow too hard to us to work in the field. Work, work, work." Most slaves lived in one-room cabins with dirt floors and a few rags for a bed. Owners wanted to keep their human property, like their animals, alive and functional, so most slaves were fed sufficiently, if not well, on salt pork, vegetables, corn mush, bread, and milk.

To escape from slavery, ⊠ Frederick Douglass disguised himself as a free sailor and took a train north from Baltimore to Philadelphia.

The treatment of slaves varied greatly. Some slaves, especially house slaves or skilled craftsmen, received relatively humane treatment. Others, at the mercy of sadistic masters or overseers, were tortured or even killed. Whipping was the most common form of discipline, administered on hundreds of different pretexts. Owners were determined to keep their slaves submissive and industrious.

One punishment in the Northern slave states was to be sold downriver to the Deep South, to Georgia, Alabama, Mississippi, or Louisiana. There, in the tropical heat of the large plantations, American slavery existed at its most brutal. Slave auctions often separated families forever. Brothers witnessed sisters exposed on the auction block; wives saw husbands led away in chains; mothers were torn away from their babies. It has been estimated that masters broke up almost a third of all slave marriages. It wasn't just the disobedient who were sold away from their friends and family. Owners routinely sold their human property to raise a little cash.

⊠ A scared-looking girl on the block in a Richmond, Virginia, slave auction.

As a slave owner explained, "They stand with us instead of money."

Some slaves tried to rebel against the system. But rebellion against the better-armed and organized white populations was doomed to failure. In 1831, a Virginia preacher named Nat Turner and a group of fellow slaves killed 57 white men, women, and children before they were captured. Whites retaliated just as savagely, killing scores of innocent blacks before hanging Turner and his followers. But such violent revolts were uncommon. Usually slaves rebelled more quietly. They broke tools, worked slowly, deliberately misunderstood instructions, or destroyed crops. The most daring tried to run away.

Generally illiterate and ignorant of the world outside their own town or plantation, most slaves could not make their way to the North without help. They depended on a group of people who were dedicated to destroying the institution of slavery and freeing the slaves. These people were called abolitionists.

Chapter Two

Am I Not a Man and a Brother?

Slave owners in the South were swimming against the tide of history. During the 19th century, the Western world slowly but finally turned against slavery. British Quakers first challenged African slavery in 1772 and succeeded in abolishing it in Great Britain. The Lord Chief Justice ruled that "every man who comes to England is entitled to the protection of English law, whatever oppression he may heretofore have suffered, and whatever may be the color of his skin." Great Britain proceeded to outlaw the slave trade in 1807 and, finally in 1833, passed the Abolition Act, which freed all slaves in British colonies. The emblem of English abolitionists was a picture of a black man in chains begging for freedom. Printed underneath him were the words: "Am I not a man and a brother?"

In the United States, too, the movement to end slavery gradually gained momentum. Quakers, who insisted that all men and women were equal in the sight of God, organized the first resistance as early as 1724. Religious opposition was a major factor in abolishing slavery in the North after the Revolutionary War. But Northern disapproval also grew as slavery spread west with the expansion of the United States.

By 1812, states were being carved out of the territory that came with

Quick Facts

★ The French revolutionary government banned slavery in the West Indian colony of Haiti in 1794. When Napoleon came to power in 1799, he tried to bring back slavery on the island. The freed blacks defeated the French troops he had sent to enslave them.

★ Prussia ended serfdom, a kind of slavery, in 1806; Austria-Hungary in 1848; and Russia in 1861.

★ The abolitionist movement made activists of many men and women who then went on to work in the women's movement. Sojourner Truth, Frederick Douglass, and William Lloyd Garrison were all early supporters of women's rights.

★ In the 50 years following the book's publication, *Uncle Tom's Cabin* was the most popular stage production in America. The character of Uncle Tom degenerated from saintly hero to submissive clown. Today, calling someone an "Uncle Tom" is considered an insult.

The famous antislavery emblem, "Am I Not a Man and a Brother?" It first appeared on British anti-slavery pamphlets and was later adopted by abolitionists in the United States.

the Louisiana Purchase of 1803. First came Louisiana, a slave state. Then Missouri applied to be admitted, also as a slave state. Northerners were dismayed. Accepting Missouri would upset the balance between slave and free states. Congressional debate became so heated that the aging Thomas Jefferson was alarmed. "In the gloomiest moment of the Revolutionary War," he wrote, "I never had any fears equal to what I feel from this source. . . . We have a wolf by the ears, and we can neither hold him nor safely let him go." Finally, Kentucky senator Henry Clay worked out a compromise.

To balance Missouri, Maine would be admitted as a free state, and a line was drawn across the Purchase at 36° 30' North latitude. Above that line, all states (except Missouri) would be free. The measure was known as the Missouri Compromise. It was just the first of many compromises that would bandage over the differences between the North and South in the years to come.

The politicians who worked out the compromises were not trying to end slavery where it already existed in the Southern states. But abolitionists were. They demanded total emancipation—immediately. As time passed—as more people were born into slavery and more territories turned into slave states—antislavery activists became angrier and angrier.

The most outspoken white abolitionist was a newspaper editor named William Lloyd Garrison. Garrison took the Declaration of Independence at its word: All men were created equal, and that included black men (and women, too). He despised all who aided and abetted slavery, from New England sea captains who transported blacks from Baltimore to the Deep South to Northern consumers who bought cloth made from Southern cotton. In January 1831, he published the first issue of an antislavery newspaper, the *Liberator*. On the first page, Garrison declared his intention: "I will be as harsh as truth, and as uncompromising as justice. . . . I am in earnest—I will not equivocate—I will not excuse—I will not retreat a single inch—AND I WILL BE HEARD!"

Heard Garrison certainly was heard. Although no issue of the *Liberator* ever had more than 3,000 copies printed, the paper was so inflammatory that the state of Georgia offered a reward of $5,000 for Garrison's arrest, and a mob in Charleston, South Carolina, burned copies of the *Liberator* in the town square. Garrison was delighted with all the publicity. He did not care how many people hated him, as long as his message got out.

Still the movement grew. Respected authors like Ralph Waldo Emerson and John Greenleaf Whittier spoke at antislavery meetings. Former slaves were often the most sought-after speakers. Frederick Douglass was the most influential African American

(Opposite, top): Antislavery leader William Lloyd Garrison spent more than 30 years fighting for the cause of abolition.

(Opposite, bottom): The cover to "The Fugitive's Song," published in 1845, which celebrates Frederick Douglass's infamous escape from slavery.

Frederick Douglass speaking in front of an audience in March 1892. Douglass was the foremost spokesman for African Americans for much of the 19th century.

of his generation. Strong, handsome, and over six feet (183 cm) tall, he could mesmerize audiences with the moving account of his life in slavery and breathtaking escape. Douglass spoke with such authority that many people could hardly believe he had once been a slave himself. His eloquent autobiography, *Narrative of the Life of Frederick Douglass*, convinced them that he had.

Sojourner Truth was another former slave who made her name on the antislavery podium. Born Isabella Hardenberg in upstate New York, Truth had seen two sisters and her mother sold away by the time she was a teenager. Three of her children were sold when she was an adult. In 1843, 16 years after enslaved New Yorkers gained their freedom, Truth began to speak at religious and antislavery meetings. She brought her story and her message of hope and faith to audiences across New England and the Midwest.

A few—a very few—Southerners dared to be abolitionists as well. Sarah and Angelina Grimké, born into a wealthy Charleston, South Carolina, family, left the South in order to speak out against the brutal acts they had witnessed. They were among the first women ever in the United States to speak publicly in front of mixed audiences of men and women. "I stand before you," Angelina said to a committee of the Massachusetts State Legislature, "to do all that I can to overturn a system . . . built upon the broken hearts and prostrate bodies of my countrymen in chains and cemented by the blood, sweat, and tears of my sisters in bonds."

⊠ Sarah Moore Grimké. She and her sister Angelina devoted their lives to the causes of abolitionism and women's rights.

At first most Northerners hated the abolitionists. White workers despised blacks, whom they suspected of trying to steal their jobs. Businessmen thought abolition was bad for business and would bring economic ruin to their Southern customers. Mobs often broke up meetings or destroyed the offices of the antislavery societies. Once a mob dragged William Lloyd Garrison through the streets of Boston with a rope around his waist, intending to lynch him. A doctor who watched the riot and Garrison's rescue by the mayor wrote, "I am an abolitionist from this very moment."

More people's feelings began to change as Congress made further compromises. The Compromise of 1850 included a new Fugitive Slave Law that forced Northerners to return runaway slaves or face imprisonment and a fine of $1,000. This enraged Northerners, who did not like to be told what to do by a bunch of Southerners. They might not have liked blacks, but they hated the bullying slave catchers who came north to catch runaways. The act turned many Northerners into abolitionists overnight.

Henry Clay argues for the ⊠ Compromise of 1850 on the floor of the Senate. The law was so controversial that the Senate debated it for more than six months.

$30 Reward.

RANAWAY from the Subscriber my Negro Woman, Betsey Merrick, with her three children Edward, Margaret Ann, and Caroline. Said Betsey is of *dark complexion*, her children are *Mulattoes.*—Her youngest is an infant.

The above reward will be given on her delivery to me, or being lodged in any jail where I can get her and her children; and an extra sum of $30 for the conviction of any white person or persons harboring them.   W. A. LANGDON.
[Wilmington (N. C.) Advertiser, Nov. 10, 1837.

⊗ This advertisement for the capture of a runaway slave and her three children was placed in the Wilmington (North Carolina) *Advertiser* in 1837.

One of the people most outraged by the situation was a quiet, absentminded writer and mother of seven. "God helping me, I will write something!" Harriet Beecher Stowe declared. "I will if I live." The novel she wrote, *Uncle Tom's Cabin*, became a runaway best-seller. Its protagonist, Uncle Tom, is a quietly heroic man, kind and religious, who is beaten to death by his owner, Simon Legree, because he will not reveal the location of two runaway girls. The novel opened the eyes of Northerners to the horrors of slavery and encouraged them to ignore the Fugitive Slave Law. The North and South were driven even farther apart.

There were many, like Stowe, who wanted to take direct action to help the slaves. The most daring actually helped slaves escape—on the Underground Railroad.

⊗ An 1899 reprint of the novel *Uncle Tom's Cabin*, depicting two of its most famous characters, Uncle Tom and his friend Little Eva.

Chapter Three

Follow the Drinking Gourd

Slaves in chains passing the Capitol. Washington, D.C., allowed slavery until 1862, although the slave trade was outlawed in 1850.

The Underground Railroad was not a railroad. It was not underground. It had no railway lines and no schedules. Yet in the 50 years before the Civil War, it helped approximately 100,000 people make their escape from slavery.

The Underground Railroad was a secret network of abolitionists who guided runaways north to safety. Its "conductors" were courageous blacks and whites who defied the law to help the escaping slaves. "Stations," run by "stationmasters," were homes, churches, barns, or caves, where runaways could rest on their journey. Almost any means of travel could be called into service as a "train": horses, rowboats, wagons with false bottoms, and even actual trains.

The destination of a runaway slave was a free state north of the

These two escaped slaves are cooks at a Union army outpost in Culpeper, Virginia.

Mason-Dixon line, where he or she could live in safety. Particularly after the Fugitive Slave Law, many thousands traveled farther north into Canada, where slave catchers had no legal right to kidnap them.

Most slaves had to make at least part of the long journey on foot. They traveled by night, hiding out in woods or swamps by day. To determine north, they followed the North Star of the Big Dipper, or "Drinking Gourd." If they heard dogs, they tried to confuse the animals by making for a stream or river.

Often runaway slaves traveled in disguise. Small men dressed as women; young women pretended to be boys. Some carried farm tools to make it look as if they were workers with a place to go and a job to do. Renowned conductor Harriet Tubman sometimes dressed as a man or as a very old woman. Once, she met her former master while she was carrying an armload of chickens. She let the chickens go and ran around wildly, trying to catch them. Amused by the comic scene, the man yelled, "Go get them, Granny!"

Quick Facts

- ★ By 1861, one third of the Southern population of 12 million were slaves; 384,000 were slave owners. Of these, only one in seven had more than 10 slaves.
- ★ Underground Railroad volunteers were of all religions: Catholic, Protestant, Jewish, and many others. The oldest synagogue in the United States, the Touro Synagogue in Newport, Rhode Island, was a station on the Underground Railroad. So was an Episcopal Parish House in Maine.
- ★ During the Civil War, Harriet Tubman worked as spy, scout, and nurse for the Union. In 1863, she led raids against Confederate plantations in South Carolina and freed nearly 800 slaves.

Secret passwords let conductors know when fugitives were expected. "Three packages will arrive on Wednesday," one conductor might signal another. A lantern in a window or a particular cloth on a clothesline let fugitives know that the coast was clear and it was safe for them to approach. Birdcalls or songs identified conductors or runaways to each other. Some songs even contained secret messages about escape routes. "Follow the Drinking Gourd," for instance, advised escapees to follow tracks made by a left foot and a peg foot along a river until they reach a place "where the great big river [the Tennessee] meets the little river [the Ohio] / Follow the drinking gourd / The old man is waiting for to take you to freedom / If you follow the drinking gourd."

There were two main routes north. Runaways who lived along the eastern shore of the United States generally headed for Philadelphia, New York, or Boston. From there they went north to upper New York State or New England. For many, the final destination was Canada, which officially refused to return fugitives to the United States in 1826.

Fugitive slaves being chased by slave hunters. After the Fugitive Slave Law of 1850, even runaway slaves who had escaped to the North were regularly hunted down, captured, or killed.

Runaways coming from the center of the country tried to make it across the Ohio River to Ohio or Indiana. Then they traveled to Detroit, Michigan, or Sandusky, Ohio, just across Lake Erie from Canada. It was nearly impossible for slaves to escape from the Deep South. Distances were too great, and antislavery sympathizers were scarce.

One of the most successful conductors on the railroad was a devout Quaker who lived on the Ohio River in Newport (now Fountain City), Indiana. Levi Coffin and his wife, Katie, helped more than 3,000 slaves escape between 1827 and 1847. John Rankin, a minister in Ripley, Ohio, also hid hundreds of fugitives in secret panels in his house on the riverbank. Another famous conductor was William Still, an African-American merchant in Philadelphia. They were just some of the roughly 3,000 men and women, black and white, who risked their lives to help the escapees.

⊠ Runaways arrive at the home of Levi and Katie Coffin on a cold winter's day.

Underground Railroad workers who were caught faced severe fines or even imprisonment. In 1833, a group of Pennsylvania Quakers were fined $4,000 when they prevented a slave owner from getting back his slave. In 1847, some Michigan abolitionists were fined $2,752 for helping six slaves escape. Some workers were thrown in jail, like Charles Torren, who was sentenced to six years for aiding runaways and died in prison. Workers could be beaten by slaveholders or threatened by mobs. When a Maryland couple was suspected of Underground Railroad activity in 1850, they were tarred and feathered and run out of town. Yet despite the many dangers of Underground Railroad work, committed abolitionists continued to follow their conscience and aid needy runaways.

The stories of the escaped slaves are suspenseful, heartbreaking, and inspiring. Luckily, some of these narratives were recorded by former slaves themselves, after they learned to read and write, or were dictated. Others were taken down by Underground Railroad workers like William Still and Levi Coffin. Following are some of the stories that have survived.

Eliza Harris

Eliza lived in Kentucky, just a few miles from the Ohio River. On the other side of the river lay Ohio and freedom. One day, Eliza heard that the very next morning she was going to be sold and separated from her two-year-old child. She gathered her child up in her arms and walked all night to the shores of the river. Since it was winter and bitterly cold, the partially frozen water was covered with swirling ice chunks. That night Eliza managed to find shelter in the home of a sympathetic couple. But the next morning, she spied slave catchers approaching the door of the house. Eliza escaped out the back and, in desperation, stepped onto a chunk of ice. The ice sank under her weight, and Eliza leaped onto another chunk. Step by step she made her way across the river on the floating sheets of ice. Sometimes she fell into the frigid water and had to place her child on an ice floe. Then she would pull herself up. The slave catchers observed her progress in amazement from the Kentucky shore. A man on the Ohio shore also watched, expecting at any moment to see her to fall in and drown.

At last, exhausted and frozen almost to death, Eliza dragged herself onto solid ground. The man who had been watching took her to the home of Reverend John Rankin, an Underground Railroad conductor in Ripley, Ohio. Rankin, in turn, sent her into Indiana, where she was sheltered by Levi and Katie Coffin. It was Katie who gave Eliza and her child their new last name: Harris. At last, helped by Underground Railroad agents along the way, Eliza and her child made their way to Chatham, Canada, to live in a settlement of former slaves.

Harriet Beecher Stowe heard the amazing story of Eliza's escape and fictionalized it in her novel *Uncle Tom's Cabin*.

✄ Harriet Beecher Stowe, the author of *Uncle Tom's Cabin*. Stowe drew on many real-life stories to depict the lives of slaves in the South.

Henry "Box" Brown

Henry Brown had an original idea. He would get a box and ship himself to freedom. He persuaded a carpenter friend in Richmond, Virginia, to build him a box about 2 x 3 x 2 1/2 feet (61 x 91 x 76 cm) with three small airholes. Then he tried to find someone who would send the box. This was difficult in Richmond, where even white people could be punished severely for helping slaves escape. But he found a sympathetic shoe dealer named Samuel A. Smith, who would ship him off as if he were sending a crate of shoes.

In March 1849, Brown climbed into the box with only a biscuit and a bit of water, and Smith nailed it shut. On one side he wrote the words THIS SIDE UP HANDLE WITH CARE. For the next day and a half, Brown was bumped, jostled, jerked around, and turned upside down. Finally the box arrived at the AntiSlavery Society of Philadelphia. Nervously the members removed the lid. The battered Brown stood up. "How do you do, gentlemen?" he said, and promptly fainted.

From then on he was known as Henry "Box" Brown. Brown told the story of his escape at antislavery meetings across the northeast until he had to move to England to escape the Fugitive Slave Law.

Ellen and William Craft

No slave escape is more thrilling than that of Ellen and William Craft. This young married couple lived in Macon, Georgia, far from any Underground Railroad network and 1,000 miles (1,609.3 km) from the North. They knew they couldn't escape by running away. So they decided to disguise themselves. Ellen, who had a light complexion, would travel as a white gentleman, and William would be her slave. She dressed in a fine black suit, with a tall black hat and green glasses to hide her eyes. Because she couldn't write, she carried her arm in a sling and pretended to have a toothache so she could wear a bandage over the lower part of her face. That way no one would see she didn't have a beard.

On December 21, 1848, Ellen and William made their "desperate leap for liberty." Ellen bought two tickets for "William Johnson and slave" at the Macon train station, and the two traveled by train and steamboat from Macon through Savannah, Georgia; Charleston, South

Carolina; Wilmington, North Carolina; Richmond and Fredericksburg, Virginia; Washington, D.C.; and Baltimore, Maryland. They had many close calls. One slave dealer even told Ellen that William looked like the kind of slave who would try to escape and offered to buy him. Ellen politely declined.

Finally, on Christmas morning, Ellen and William Craft arrived in Philadelphia. The story of their spectacular escape made them instantly famous in antislavery circles. They moved to England, where they lived for 20 years and raised a family. After the Civil War, they came back to Savannah, where Ellen opened a freedman's school. They lived to a happy old age, surrounded by a large family and many friends.

William Wells Brown

William was born in Kentucky in 1814, the son of a slave woman and his master's brother. By the time he was a teenager, William had lost all six of his siblings, who had either died or been sold away. He and his mother made a reckless try for freedom but were caught by slave catchers. As punishment, his mother was sold downriver to New Orleans. Her last words to him were "Now try to get your liberty!"

By now William was owned by a steamboat captain on the Mississippi River. On December 31, 1831, the boat was docked in Cincinnati, Ohio. William walked off the boat carrying someone else's trunk and never looked back. He hid in some woods until it was night, then started to walk, following the North Star. But it was winter and very cold, and William had no overcoat and little food. He nearly froze to death before an elderly Quaker man spied him and took him home. It was many weeks before William was strong enough to travel again. When he was about to leave, he asked the kind couple to give him a proper name.

"If I name thee," the man said, "I shall call thee Wells Brown after myself."

About a week later, William Wells Brown reached Cleveland. Here he stayed, working for a steamboat company and becoming a conductor on the Underground Railroad. Later he moved to Boston, learned to read and write, and lectured about slavery in America and Europe.

William Wells Brown was a gifted author. His autobiographical narrative, *William Wells Brown, A Fugitive Slave* (1847), made him famous. He also wrote the first novel published by an African-American author, *Clotel; or the President's Daughter* (1853). He wrote the first play, too. Yet despite his success, for the rest of his life William Wells Brown remained haunted by the memory of his lost mother and family. He died in 1884, having never seen them again.

Ann Maria Weems

Ann Maria Weems was a 15-year-old girl who escaped from slavery by herself, but she couldn't have done it without her friends in the Underground Railroad. Ann Maria, who lived near Rockville, Maryland, was the property of a slave trader named Charles Price. An abolitionist lawyer in Washington, D.C., named J. Bigelow bought her sister and mother in order to free them. In turn, Ann Maria's mother saved enough money to buy her brother. But Price wouldn't part with Ann Maria. So Bigelow concocted a plan.

Ann Maria managed to slip away from the Price home and came to Washington, D.C. Bigelow hid her for six weeks until the hunt died down. Then he disguised her as a young male carriage driver named Joe Wright from York, Pennsylvania, and left her in the care of a friend, Dr. H. Ann Maria drove Dr. H and his carriage down the streets of the city, through Maryland, and into Philadelphia. There they stopped at the home of free black abolitionist William Still. Still transported her farther north to the Underground Railroad station of Lewis Tappan in Brooklyn. Since it was late November, Ann Maria had two Thanksgiving dinners—one at the Stills "and one at the Tappans."

Then it was time for the final leg of her journey. A black minister from Brooklyn traveled with the girl up to Chatham, Canada, where Ann Maria's aunt and uncle lived. Their reunion was joyful. "Ann Maria, is that you?" the aunt cried out when she saw her. "Thank God, you are free!"

Solomon Northrup

Kidnapped and sold into slavery, Solomon Northrup lost his identity and his freedom at the same time. It was a fate that befell many free blacks in the years before the Civil War.

Solomon Northrup grew up in Minerva, a small town in upstate New York. His father was the freed ex-slave of a man named Northrup. His mother had always been free, and so was Solomon. He was an intelligent, likable, and talented boy who loved to play the fiddle at neighborhood dances. In 1829, he married and settled in Saratoga Springs, where he and his wife had three children.

One day in 1841, two men approached him about taking a job in a small traveling circus. Delighted at the chance to make some extra money, Solomon traveled with them to Albany and New York City, then all the way down to Washington, D.C. This was a mistake on Solomon's part, since Washington was a slaveholding district and still held slave auctions. Sure enough, Solomon was drugged by his supposed friends and woke up to find himself shackled to a bench in the slave pen.

Protesting, he told the slave dealer he was a free man named Solomon Northrup, and he was beaten almost to death.

Solomon, now called Platt, was shipped downriver to New Orleans and sold. For the next 12 years, he was owned by three different men and humiliated, whipped, and forced to labor in sugar cane and cotton fields. Finally, he found a Canadian handyman with abolitionist sympathies who was willing to write letters to Northrup's friends and family in Saratoga. When she discovered where her husband was, Solomon's wife, Anne, wrote to the governor of New York, who in turn appointed a lawyer named Henry B. Northrup to see to the case. Henry B. Northrup was related to the man who had owned Solomon's father, and he already knew Solomon. He set off for Marksville, Louisiana, on a rescue mission.

On the day in 1853 when Henry Northrup arrived at the plantation with the papers declaring him to be a free man, Solomon was so overcome with joy and relief that he fainted. Solomon Northrup lived to be reunited with his family and to write a book, *Twelve Years a Slave*.

The indomitable Harriet ⊠ Tubman, famed conductor on the Underground Railroad.

Harriet Tubman

Harriet Tubman was the most famous of all the conductors on the Underground Railroad. In the 10 years preceding the Civil War, she helped more than 300 slaves escape to freedom. "On my underground railroad I never ran my train off the track and I never lost a passenger," she boasted.

Harriet was born into slavery on a plantation on the eastern shore of Maryland. One evening, when she was 28, she heard a rumor that she was about to be sold. She decided to escape. "There were two things I had a right to," she decided, "Liberty and Death. If I could not have one, I would have the other, for no man should take me alive." Her journey took her from one Underground Railroad hiding place to another: the attic of a Quaker farm, the barn of a German family, the potato cellar in the cabin of a free black family. Finally she reached Philadelphia, where she found work as a hotel cook.

Tubman was free, but her family wasn't. She returned to the South 19 times to rescue her sister, her brothers, her parents, and many others. Even with a $40,000 bounty on her head, Tubman made her daring journey twice a year until the Civil War broke out. For her indomitable courage in leading her people out of slavery and into the promised land of freedom, she became known as the Moses of her people.

Laborers unload and ship Federal supplies on a Virginia wharf. Blacks joined the Union cause as spies, scouts, laborers, and finally soldiers when the Civil War started.

Chapter Four

Free at Last

★ In April 1862, Congress freed the slaves in the District of Columbia. Slave owners were paid $300 for each freed individual.

★ In June 1862, Congress freed all slaves in the territories. On January 1, 1863, the Emancipation Proclamation freed slaves in the rebellious states: Virginia, North Carolina, South Carolina, Georgia, Florida, Alabama, Mississippi, Louisiana, Arkansas, Tennessee, and Texas. The 13th Amendment freed the slaves in the remaining slave states (border states): Missouri, Kentucky, Maryland, and Delaware.

★ Sixteen African-American soldiers received the Congressional Medal of Honor for service in the Union army.

During the 1850s, the nation moved toward war. North-South relations, already strained by the Fugitive Slave Law, worsened with the passage of the Kansas-Nebraska Act in 1854. This act allowed settlers in the territories of Kansas and Nebraska to decide for themselves whether they should live in free or slave states, thereby overthrowing the Missouri Compromise, which had forbidden slavery in those territories. Settlers who moved into Kansas from the North and South quickly turned the territory into a war zone. Proslavery "Border Ruffians" burned farms, destroyed homes, and ambushed antislavery settlers. In retaliation, an abolitionist named John Brown led an antislavery gang on a midnight raid to murder five proslavery settlers in their beds. In the end, the violence took the lives of more than 200 people, and the territory became known as Bleeding Kansas.

✉ John Brown, a fanatical abolitionist who turned to violence to end slavery.

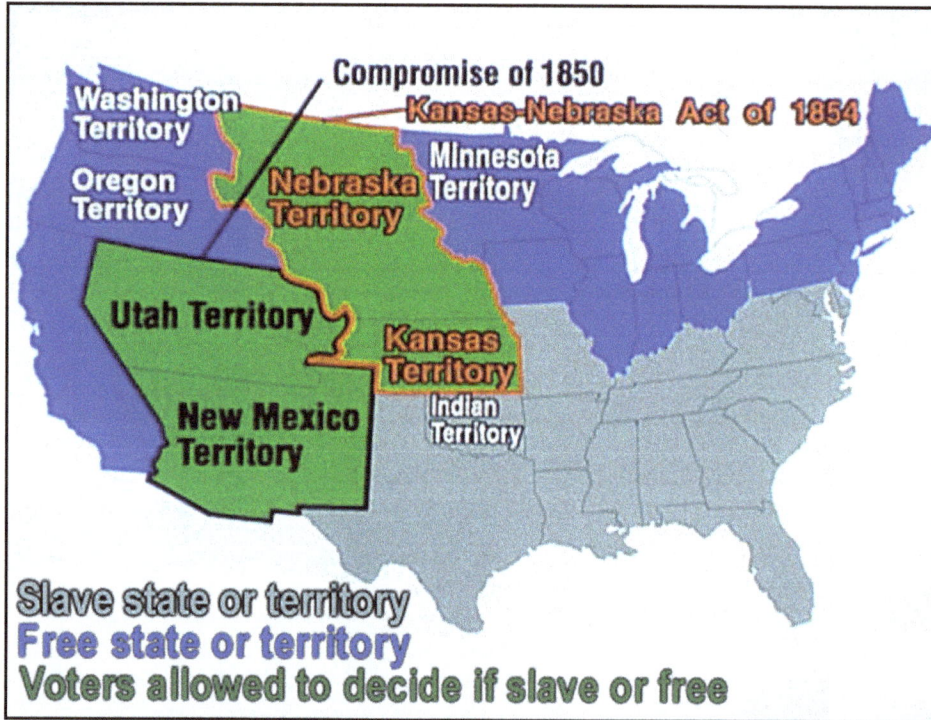

Compromise of 1850
Kansas-Nebraska Act of 1854

Washington Territory
Oregon Territory
Minnesota Territory
Nebraska Territory
Utah Territory
Kansas Territory
New Mexico Territory
Indian Territory

Slave state or territory
Free state or territory
Voters allowed to decide if slave or free

This map shows the spread of slavery into the territories by 1854. The Compromise of 1850 allowed settlers in the Utah and New Mexico territories to decide the issue of slavery by popular sovereignty. According to the Missouri Compromise (1820), slavery was permitted only in territories south of latitude 36° 30'N, except for Missouri. By allowing settlers in the Kansas and Nebraska territories above that imaginary line to decide for themselves whether they wanted slavery, the Kansas-Nebraska Act of 1854 overturned the Missouri Compromise. Nebraska eventually voted to remain free. Kansas erupted into violence over the issue.

Two days after the Kansas-Nebraska Act was passed, a fugitive named Anthony Burns was kidnapped by slave catchers in Boston. Enraged citizens took to the streets, protesting Burns's imprisonment and return down south. Funeral bells tolled and the crowd cried "Shame! Shame!" as Burns was led away in chains. In the end, it took 1,000 Boston policemen and almost $100,000 of public money to return Burns to slavery.

As antislavery feelings grew, violence burst forth a number of times in Congress. Massachusetts senator Charles Sumner was beaten almost to death by a Southern Congressman because of his antislavery remarks.

In 1857, the Dred Scott decision brought matters to a head. Dred Scott was a slave who had lived with his master in free territory before

THE ESCAPE ON SHIPBOARD.

ARREST IN BOSTON.

DEPARTURE FROM BOSTON.

THE SALE.

THE ADDRESS.

AUCTION

THE PRISON.

Anthony Burns

A portrait of fugitive slave Anthony Burns surrounded by scenes from his life, beginning with his sale at auction and ending with his imprisonment.

returning to Missouri. With the help of antislavery lawyers, he sued for his freedom. The case reached the Supreme Court. There justices ruled that blacks had never been citizens of the United States and "were so far inferior that they had no rights which a white man was bound to respect." Slaves were property and their owners could take them anywhere in the free states. Furthermore, "Congress had no power to abolish or prevent slavery in any of the territories." In other words, the Missouri Compromise was declared unconstitutional.

Indignant citizens from the Democratic and Whig Parties formed the new Republican Party, determined to keep slavery out of the West. In the election of 1860, Republican Abraham Lincoln became president—and within months, the Civil War began.

The Underground Railroad became busier than ever. With Southern white men called to serve the Confederacy, slaves by the thousands took advantage of their masters' absences to slip away to the North. As the war went on, slaves departed en masse from the border

⊠ Dred Scott and his wife Harriet Scott. Scott sued for his freedom after living in a territory where slavery was illegal.

states of Missouri, Kentucky, Tennessee, and Maryland. At first, most slaves who appeared behind Federal lines were returned to their masters under the Fugitive Slave Law. But soon Northern officers realized it was to the North's advantage to deprive Confederates of their "property." In 1861, Union general Benjamin Butler, the commander of Fortress Monroe in Virginia, put three runaway slaves to work in the camp. When the owner's agent appeared to take them back, Butler told him he was confiscating the runaways as property of war. Within a month the fortress was flooded with thousands of "contraband," as the runaways were called.

Former slaves follow Union soldiers in North Carolina. Many slaves fled from their owners whenever a Northern army was nearby.

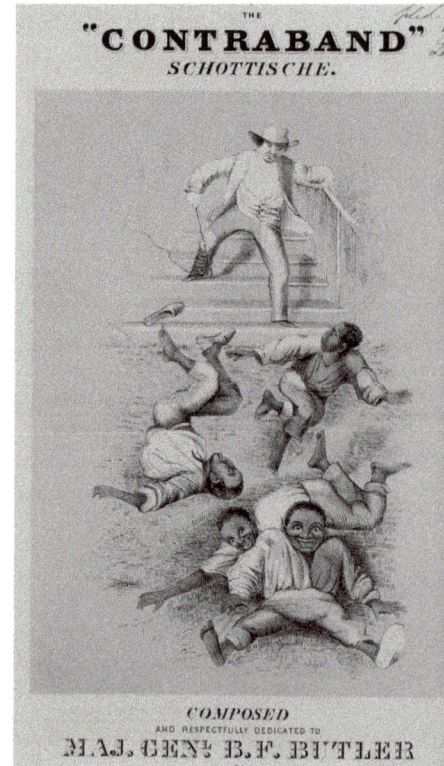

"CONTRABAND"
SCHOTTISCHE.

COMPOSED
AND RESPECTFULLY DEDICATED TO
MAJ. GEN! B. F. BUTLER

Soon, wherever they went in Tennessee, in Georgia, or in Alabama, Union armies were followed by floods of fugitives—men, women, and children. Commanders learned to put the contraband to work, building bridges and fortifications and performing a variety of military chores. They were neither slave nor free, but more and more Northern soldiers saw that they were useful.

January 1, 1863, was the day the slaves had longed for. That morning, Lincoln signed the final Emancipation Proclamation and freed one million slaves in the rebellious states. Throughout the South and behind the Union lines, free men and women celebrated their deliverance. Frederick Douglass was in Boston's Tremont Temple with

※ This group of contrabands in Virginia escaped behind Union lines and freed themselves.

※ A song sheet for the "Contraband Schottische" shows slaves gleefully escaping from their owner. A "schottische" is a kind of dance.

hundreds of other abolitionists when the proclamation was issued. With one accord the congregation rose and sang, "Sound the loud timbrel o'er Egypt's dark sea / Jehovah hath triumphed, his people are free."

Slavery was not yet vanquished. But its end was near. After the Emancipation, some 200,000 black troops were recruited to serve in the Union army. There they proved that black soldiers could fight as well and as bravely as their white counterparts. One member of the North Carolina Colored Volunteers, Joseph E. Williams, wrote: "For this cause we will fight, for the cause of freedom. I will draw my sword against my oppressor and the oppressors of my race. . . . And I will sacrifice everything in order to save the gift of freedom for my race."

Fugitives crossing the ✉ Rappahannock River in Virginia to seek the protection of the Union Army.

On December 6, 1865, the U.S. Congress ratified the 13th Amendment to the Constitution, freeing all remaining slaves in the land: "Neither slavery nor involuntary servitude, except as a punishment for crime whereof the party shall have been duly convicted, shall exist within the United States, or any place subject to their jurisdiction."

A few weeks later, on December 29, William Lloyd Garrison closed the offices of the *Liberator* in Boston. There was no more need for an abolitionist movement, an antislavery newspaper, or the Underground Railroad. The great battle against American slavery had been won.

Members of company E of the 4th U.S. Colored Infantry at Fort Lincoln in Washington, D.C. Black men were proud finally to be allowed to serve in the Union army.

Further Reading

Douglass, Frederick. *Narrative of the Life of Frederick Douglass, an American Slave*. New York: Penguin, 1982.

Fradin, Dennis Brindell. *Bound for the North Star: True Stories of Fugitive Slaves*. New York: Clarion Books, 2000.

Gorrell, Gena K. *North Star to Freedom: The Story of the Underground Railroad*. New York: Delacorte Press, 1996.

Haskins, Jim. *Get on Board: The Story of the Underground Railroad*. New York: Scholastic, 1993.

Petry, Ann. *Harriet Tubman: Conductor on the Underground Railroad*. New York: HarperTrophy, 1996.

Stowe, Harriet Beecher. *Uncle Tom's Cabin, or Life Among the Lowly*. New York: Literary Classics of the United States, 1982.

Winter, Jeanette. *Follow the Drinking Gourd*. New York: Knopf, 1992.

Glossary

Abolition—The act of abolishing, or getting rid of, slavery.

Border States—Slave states, such as Kentucky, Maryland, Delaware, and Missouri, that bordered the Union and did not join the Confederacy.

Compromise of 1850—A Congressional compromise that admitted California to the Union as a free state, allowed popular sovereignty in the territories of New Mexico and Utah, banned the slave trade in Washington, D.C., and passed a strict fugitive slave law.

Confederate—A person who was a citizen of the Confederate States of America.

Confederate States of America—The name of the nation formed by the 11 states that seceded from the United States in 1860 and 1861.

Constitutional Convention (1787)—The meeting of delegates in Philadelphia who wrote a constitution for the United States.

Contraband—A slave who escaped across Union lines during the Civil War.

Cotton gin—A machine invented by Eli Whitney in 1793 to clean cotton fibers.

Dred Scott Decision (1857)—A Supreme Court decision that stated that slaves were property even in free states.

Emancipation Proclamation (1863)—President Lincoln's declaration freeing the slaves in the Confederacy.

Freedman's Bureau—The government agency established to help former slaves.

Fugitive Slave Law of 1850—The act of Congress that ordered all citizens to return runaway slaves.

Gettysburg Address (1863)—The speech given by President Lincoln after the Battle of Gettysburg.

Kansas-Nebraska Act (1854)—The law that divided Nebraska into two territories and stated that the question of slavery would be decided by popular sovereignty.

Louisiana Purchase (1803)—President Thomas Jefferson's purchase of the huge Louisiana Territory from Napoleon Bonaparte.

Mason-Dixon Line—Imaginary line between the Northern and Southern states.

Medal of Honor—The highest military award in the United States.

Missouri Compromise (1820)—A Congressional plan to keep the number of slave and free states equal.

Paddy Rollers—The name given by slaves to the patrollers who tried to prevent slaves from escaping from Southern plantations.

Secede—To withdraw from or leave an organization.

Secessionist—In the Civil War, someone who believed in the right of a state to separate from the United States.

Slave Codes—Oppressive laws that restricted the rights of slaves.

Slavery—The state of one person being owned by another.

Underground Railroad—The secret network of people that helped slaves escape from slavery.

Union—During the Civil War, the states that did not secede from the United States of America.

Whig—The American political party formed in 1834 that was followed by the Republican Party.

Index

www.ingramcontent.com/pod-product-compliance
Lightning Source LLC
Chambersburg PA
CBHW040853100426

42813CB00015B/2794